Robyn's Verse

Robyn's Verse

Robyn Wallace Kilpatrick

Compiled by Scott Ethan Kilpatrick

Copyright ©2001 by Scott Ethan Kilpatrick.

Library of Congress Number: 2001118956
ISBN #:   Hardcover   1-4010-3309-1
                Softcover   1-4010-3308-3

All rights reserved. No part of this book may be reproduced or transmitted in any form or by any means, electronic or mechanical, including photocopying, recording, or by any information storage and retrieval system, without permission in writing from the copyright owner.

This book was printed in the United States of America.

To order additional copies of this book, contact:
Xlibris Corporation
1-888-7-XLIBRIS
www.Xlibris.com
Orders@Xlibris.com

Contents

Preface 13

POEMS

On a Clearer Day 23
You Know Not Joy 24
Broken Thread 25
The Struggle 27
A Prelude to Sleep 28
In Remembrance 30
Nature's Painted Cup 31
Relief 33
I Will Hold You in My Heart 34
Looking Back 36
You Carry It with You 37
Knowing 39
Just Once Around 40
Just Emotion 42
An Island in My Mind 43
Illusion 45
Introspective 46
His Slumber 48
If 49
Gravity 50
Inspiration 51
Freedom 52
Extremes 53
Forgiveness 54

Don't Dare Say You Care 55
Doubt 57
Experience 58
A Step at a Time 59
A Pivotal Point 61
A Tree before a Fall 62
For Your Recovery 63
An Altered State of Mind 64
A Window in My Mind 66
Be Objective 67
A Woman Now 69
Before 70
Absentia 72
The Blessing 73
A Blessing In Disguise 74
Admittance: A Dawning 76
Broken Memory 77
A Cup of Poetry 79
Creator of My Doom 80
I'll wait 81
Denial 82
Fragments 84
In the Rain 85
Focus! 87
I Will Not 88
Face to Face 89
Fear and Darkness 90
Exposure 92
Mystery of Me 93
On Order 94
No Longer 95
No More 96
No Chance 97
Will I? 98
My Destiny 99

Pray and Fight	100
Do You	101
I Picture It	102
Food for Thought	103
A Noble Prize	104
Our Choice	106
I Learned	107
Perspective	108
Wouldn't Blame You	109
A Star	111
Letting Go	112
Mercy	114
Movin' Along	115
Without You	116
Loneliness	117
A Diversion	118
Not the Average Kind	119
Ponderance	120
Real Joy	121
Premonition	123
Rain Song	124
Resolve	125
Remnants	126
Validation	127
Vain Whisperings	128
Resistance	130
Peaceful Pathways	131
Poetic Ways	133
Poetic Ways 2	134
Poetry Man	136
Poetry	137
Riddance	139
Portrait	140
Real Living	141
The Confines	142

Resentment	144
The Culminating Point	145
The Living	147
The Only Key	148
Waiting	149
You Can	150
You Get Me High	151
The Young Heart	153
The Written Word	154
Timeless	155
To Regard Circumstance	156
Sea of Me	157
The Wine	158
Sent Away	160
Revelation	161
Sense of Loss	163
Sunlight	164
Societal Prejudice	166
That Steely Trap	167
Something to Gain	169
Unexpected	170
Unheard	172
Upon the Slate	173
My Gift	175
His Gift	176
Love Wasted	177
Love That Can	179
An Undue Chore	181
An Impregnable Force	182
Given Awhile	184
Longing for Home	186
Had Not Seen You	187
Love's Respite	189
Enslaved	190
Transition	191

Winds Whisper Your Name 192
A Hard Stance 193
Dangerous 194
Unavailable 196
Uncertainty 197
What Do I Do? 198
Where is the Hope? 199
The Beautiful, The Lonely 200
Looking for Me 201
Desire 202
Sudden Hush 203
I Imagine 204
With His Eyes 205
Anticipation 206
Beauty 207
I Learned of You 208
It's Over 210
Martha 211
You Come to Me 212
You Must Be of God 213
Touched by Fate 214
The Pain 215
A Call to Harvest 216
Where the Birds Are 217
Resolution 219
My Gift of Words for Always 220

SHORT STORIES

The Illumination 225
A Time to Rejoice 229
Work Cited 232

*Dedicated to all who've loved and lost...
and yet press on*

Preface

Those people who impact our lives the most are not the movie stars, entertainers, or even the politicians but are the few who dare to love and give of themselves so very completely and freely. They are instruments of God's grace. Although tossed into a large river, these seemingly insignificant pebbles create waves and ripples, touching all of those fortunate enough to be near them. And we receive it, even though it is, by its very nature, undeserved. They float into our lives with the grace and beauty of a butterfly, hovering momentarily before continuing onto their destination. We are sorry to see them leave but know we have been blessed by their presence and, somehow, this is enough.

The contents of this book represent a compilation of poetry, encompassing a portion of the 1980s and 1990s, spanning most of Robyn's adult life. It seems that, when inspiration occurred, Robyn sought any number of immediately available objects for documenting her thoughts, including napkins, stationary, and even airline "throw-up" bags. Ultimately, she would faithfully re-write the verses on standard paper. We often talked of publishing her poems and even purchased books regarding the process of publishing poetry. But the weeks, months, and years rolled by . . . and now I find myself alone with only her pictures and words keeping me company. What follows is Robyn's autobiography (in her own words), portions of which she used for her application autobiographical essay to Salem College.

Into an environment of passion, rage, drama, hellfire and brimstone I was born. Into a world of words that fascinated me, serenaded me, and dictated to me how I must live and how much of myself I must give, I arrived.

I was born in Wadesboro, North Carolina, on February 18, 1965, three days before Malcolm X was gunned down in New York and on the same birth month and day as the Nobel Prize winning novelist, Toni Morrison. The heat of the southern Bible-belt held plenty of room for a theatre manager, turned furniture salesman father. After moving his family to High Point and then to Winston-Salem, North Carolina, my father found his calling in the ministry.

At the age of three I welcomed into the world my little brother. Salem Baptist Day School seemed the most appropriate place for my brother and I to attend. There, until the ninth grade, I received a wonderful education in an atmosphere, which, though sheltered, offered an escape from the extremely legalistic one at home. Self expression was limited to rare and legalism was the rule in our household. How well I remember watching the Jackson 5 perform before the Queen of England only to be interrupted by brutal discipline for my secular interest (because to "spare the rod" certainly would "spoil the child").

Upon my sophomore year of high school I was allowed to enter the public school system where I attended Mount Tabor High School. There, I flourished in English and drama. My junior and senior years were spent at R.J. Reynolds High School pursuing these same interests. The year of my graduation was also the year of my devastation. Nineteen hundred and eighty-three brought both triumph and pain, as I witnessed the disintegration of my family. I was left to work odd jobs only to dream about college.

Upon the break-up and dissolution of our family unit at my young age of 17, I grasped inward for a seemingly controlled self-image to portray to the world, one with which to shield my pain, to hide the tears that threatened me and to close out the screams that were deafeningly close. For years, I pretended to have succeeded and I suppose that I fooled no one but myself. The happiest years of my life have followed my coming to know myself through my own tears, my rage, my laughter, joy and pain, and my ability to tell the truth, unabashed and unashamed.

On February 4, 1985, I decided to spread my wings on the horizon of my dreams. Piedmont Airlines hired a nineteen-year-old woman-child with dreams to see something beyond backyards and Bible-belt. I remained employed in the airline industry for ten years. During my tenure, not only did I discover other destinations, but I discovered myself. Through poetry and facing the pain of my past, I was able to further pursue my ultimate ambitions including unconditional love, happiness, family, education, self expression and actualization. Therefore, poetry was my freedom in its truest sense, the wings with which my soul takes flight.

Nineteen ninety-three was indeed a great year of strength and struggle, for strength without failure, both physically and psychologically. Nineteen ninety-three brought in a loving relationship, certainly unconventional and untraditional, yet one which provided a medium through which growth could be attained and transition proceeded; transition which allowed confrontation, allowed a truth in judgment to be realized and to be called. Many judgment calls were indeed made and decisions followed, allowing necessary doors to be closed and lines and boundaries to be drawn, both in personal relationships and everyday relationships. Through this process came the ability to value the self as having worth, worthy of respect and consideration, and the ability to judge some circumstances and people unworthy of consideration.

Physical goals and dedication ruled as one of the foremost mediums through which personal growth and satisfaction could be realized. Charts were kept on training and aerobic workouts. The summer days brought running as an excellent way to exert stress and tension as well as to build endurance and self esteem.

Finally, and one of the most important things 1993 issued in was closure—closure on the past, on relationships. I met an answer to a prayer, long prayed subconsciously, when I finally voiced my prayer aloud, in sincerity, and carried out a relationship the way God would have me conduct it. I got engaged December 8, 1993. Who would have ever thought it? But God sent it.

On May 21, 1994, I was married in my hometown after a fairy tale romance, engagement, and wedding.

>Dearest Scott,
>
>A sudden sense of urgency
>As never felt before
>Compels me—an emergency—
>To tell you so much more.
>
>An open door, an open book
>To my heart, to my life
>And there you stand—
>You take me as your lady—
>Soon your wife.
>
>Hand in hand we'll travel down
>Such roads we've never before
>Alone we've known, experienced;
>Together, so much more.
>
>Robyn

Following our marriage, Robyn and I moved to Rochester, Minnesota, as I completed a surgical pathology fellowship at the Mayo Clinic. After a lot of soul-searching, Robyn left her job as a USAir flight attendant and worked as an assistant manager of a Limited clothing store at a local mall. In June of 1995, we moved back to Winston-Salem, and I took a position on staff at Wake Forest University Baptist Medical Center. Life was not easy at first. Paying off student loans and other debt we had accumulated took its toll on our finances, leaving precious little for

Robyn's education. But as with everything, she accepted the setback and started down another road, successfully selling cosmetics with Mary Kay.

What impressed me most about Robyn was the fact that nothing in life was beneath her . . . conversely, I considered Robyn above everything and everyone else! I took the job and career with the prestige; Robyn chose the harder road, selling cosmetics for Mary Kay Cosmetics and handing out her business cards at malls and to anyone who would listen. In general, people were always more interested in what I was doing. Yet, this never stopped Robyn. Sure, she got discouraged but her drive was incredible. And she did everything wholeheartedly. With Mary Kay, she won seemingly innumerable awards, including a company car, a fiery red Grand Am! Once we became financially stable (Spring, 1997), I encouraged Robyn to go to college. This had always been her lifelong dream but, unlike myself, who had all the opportunities, she was forced to patiently put this dream aside. By the time she attended college (first at Salem College and later at University of North Carolina), Robyn was 32 years old. Not surprisingly, she was immediately a straight "A" student. She attended Salem College for less than a year before we moved to Chapel Hill in March, 1998. Although not well known among most of my colleagues, it was Robyn who encouraged me to look at an available position at the University of North Carolina and it was Robyn who, after my 3 interviews, was initially sure that our destiny lay in Chapel Hill. Nevertheless, life was never easy for Robyn. She struggled with friendships at UNC . . . being a non-traditional, older student, she had a distinct feeling of loneliness, which she shared with me on many occasions. It was difficult for a married 35-year-old woman to relate to 18, 19, and 20-year-old college students. Yet, she pressed on. I, on the other hand, enjoyed very rich professional relationships with my colleagues. Interestingly, this never resulted in any resentment from Robyn . . . she always shared in my joys and successes. But our romance and her life was tragically cut short. On October 17, 2000, Robyn died in an automobile accident. Yes, from a strict earthly perspective, I took the high road in life and Robyn took the low road . . . and in God's kingdom the humble low road leads to a throne!

As I have sorted through our past and belongings, I came across some of the cards that we had sent each other during our short time together. The most significant was the first card. Robyn and I were engaged on the evening of December 8, 1993; I proposed to her "on bended knee" in a restaurant in Winston-Salem, the Zeveley House. She accepted my offer, handing me a card (the card had a painting by Auguste Renoir, *A GIRL WITH A WATERING CAN*) but, most importantly, contained a poem she had written,

The Gift of Love
Your love—to me—a present,
A symbol, shining brightly
    I shall wear.
Not to be taken lightly
    Yet you dare bestow it!
And the answer—"Yes!"
    I know it. I am sure.
For our love is true and pure,
    And effervescent!
And your love, to me—
    A present.

Robyn's love to me was a present . . . and I give it back to you.

Dear Robyn,

God gave you to me for a short while and for this I am so grateful. I loved you more than life itself. You were my best friend and my lover. Thank you for being a part of my life. Thank you for improving me as a person. Thank you most of all for loving all of me, even though I never deserved it.

God has taken you home to be with Him. Although I miss you unbearably, I will rejoice in your new life, as I know we will ultimately be together again. Half of me has died but half of you has survived. It is truly better to have loved you and lost you than to have never loved you at all.

Good night sweetheart . . . I'll see you in the morning.

Scott

POEMS

On a Clearer Day

Words written.
Thoughts hidden.
Letters that I've put away.
Words I've chosen not to say.

Yet this does not mean
My thoughts are but a dream
Nor that I do not feel them.

But rather,
I conceal them.

Maybe on some sunny day—
These letters I have put away—
I'll bring them out—
On a clearer day of lesser doubt.

On a clearer day without so many
Clouds
Hung in the sky.

On a day without so much
Hurt
To deny.

And I'll give them all to you—
Each letter I treasure—
To do with, what you will do,
For I'll be feeling better.

You Know Not Joy

Cold and lifeless lips of plaster;
Heart, as hard as alabaster.
Grey and dull, unflinching, passive eyes
Reveal neither the truth, nor lies.

How very hard it is to reach you.
With my words would I beseech you
But I find all effort to be vain.
For you know not joy, you know not pain.

Broken Thread

The antiquated rocker
Keeping rhythm as she sang
Seemed but filler for the silence
Of the phone that never rang.

Sunlight setting into evening,
Hands once clenched are now remiss,
Expressionless,
Surrendering this vacuum.

This abyss seems to send her ever spinning
Through the chasm of her dread
And the air is ever thinning Life—
As fragile as a thread

Any moment to be broken—
Leaves her barely hanging on
'Til the words she once had spoken
Lay suspended in the dawn.

The antiquated rocker
Cannot keep her rhythm long.
Air is lighter, ever quieter
With the absence of her song.

No more will she pine away
For loved ones to arrive.
The chime holds no significance.
The toll, approaching four and five

And six and seven
Earth has little to afford,
For her sights are set on heaven.
She has gone to see her Lord.

And the angels are rejoicing
With the new song that she sings.
Broken thread, no more to dread
The phone that never rings.

The Struggle

I fight
because I am free.

I am free
because I'm happy
to be me.

A Prelude to Sleep

My body longs for sleep—
But for my mind, sleep never comes.
My body tosses, turns,
And my thoughts, on the run,

Constantly are contemplating possibilities
As I search for answers
To the questions
Asked of me . . .

A multitude of questions!
It's as if another person
Harasses, interrogates,
For I can't draw a curtain,

Pull a shade, or close a blind.
Is there a way to shield my mind?
Unaware of answers—
Peaceful sleep I cannot find!

Questions, growing,
Growing like a cancer
For which there is no cure—
Nor is there an answer!

I wonder how I'll stay the night—
Or if I will endure.
Can I continue at this pace,
Uncertain and unsure?

For I am slowly wearing down.
Maybe now to rest my head.
Perhaps a resting place I've found—
Here, in the comfort of my bed.

A single hour of rest
Should not seem so great a quest.
I hope for later this will keep,
For now my body longs to sleep.

In Remembrance

In my travels my subconscious mind unravels
Like a spool letting loose of all its thread.
Like the graves letting loose of all their dead
In resurrection—

I find moments of reflection
Tend to summer seasons, days of rain,
And my mind no longer minds to feel the pain
In remembrance.

Nature's Painted Cup

A bending branch, a budding rose—
If loss of sight then I suppose
We'd search within our memory
These visions in our minds to see . . .

A flower, a daisy
The beauty of the field!
A willow blowing in the wind
As I am standing still.

Behold this in your passing.
Stop there in your tracks!
Take some time to look around
For you may not be back!

Water trickling—Hidden stream—
A lovely little pond!
So much to be discovered
If you'll only love beyond

Your single glance, and hurried look.
Just one brief moment you took
To drink from nature's painted cup—
To find your spirit lifted up

Has made life seem worth all the while!
Take example from the child
You saw today, that child at play.
Throw your useless worry away!

A bending branch, a budding rose—
If loss of sight then I suppose
We'd search within our memory
These visions in our minds to see.

But minds run dry if you and I
Continue to be passers by.
So much beauty nature holds—
Leaves of crimson, jade and gold!

Jagged peaks, a rugged cliff—
Capture it! Now set adrift
A rugged ocean, foamy sea.
Plant it in your memory.
For minds run dry if you and I
Continue to be passers by.
It's there for us to stop and sup—
To drink from nature's painted cup.

Relief

I came to see you
To tell you
Life
Is smiling on me.

Many changes in motion—
Things
I can't even see.

The Importance of it all
Is, finally,
Now I am free.

Funny how love changes.
We're now merely strangers,
and Life is smiling on me.

I Will Hold You in My Heart

It is but for a season I see carved into your face
Many signs and lines and seasons, and the years that slowly trace
A miracle of furrows, deepened ever by your sorrow.
Once you stood and held within your hand the promise of tomorrow.

*

All your days have been fulfilling, and now life is ever stilling,
Stilling ever, all the whisperings of ravage, and rasping breath.
And I watch, as eyes are filling, filling ever with your chilling
As your life is ever spilling, spilling over into death.

*

If I could once more hold you, much the way I used to hold you—
If I somehow could have told you how you are my everything . . .
But in death my love's forsaken, and death my chance has taken—
Taken every chance for fighting with the biting of its sting.

*

It is but for a reason I see signs and lines and seasons.
Life once held you as an easel, and you, my love, a work of art,
Tell me now that you are leaving. Still you find it ever pleasing—
Pleasing ever, that forever I will hold you in my heart.

*

I watch, as death, foreboding, stands above you, ever gloating—
Gloating ever as it's smitten on your forehead a dark kiss.
I know your death is nearing. I can feel it. It is searing.
It is death reducing fearing into something such as this:

*

That I should stand forsaken. Left to stand as Life is taken,
Taken ever by the maker who created all my bliss.
I stand left holding, holding ever what you told me.
For you told me how it pleases you I hold you in my heart.

*

So this day 'til forever, you are finding that I ever
Carry you in each endeavor. I will never let you part.

Looking Back

I turn around
And all these years
Are gone.

Just a yawn
In life's history
... Is my life missing
me?

You Carry It with You

You carry it with you—
Like some loss;
A sore
Hidden beneath a sleeve.

A scabbing over—
At all costs;
A hand
Covers the mouth that grieves.

You carry it with you.

You deny the tears you cry
As if they are not falling
A blotting out; the midnight sky
In darkness finds you crawling.

And though you push it far away
The pain, in reappearing,
Reveals itself—an inner wound
The flesh itself is tearing!

Still, you carry it with you—
Like some loss;
A sore
Hidden beneath a sleeve.

The stifled cry
You well disguise

ROBYN WALLACE KILPATRICK

The pain
That never leaves.

You carry it with you.

Knowing

A crass indictment—
A life void of excitement,

Emptiness, never felt before . . .
Knowing you aren't in my life anymore.

Just Once Around

Just once around and so my goal—
To live my life, take control.
Live each day as if it were the last.

Persevere. Endure. To fight against all odds,
My wrongs I'll right
And relinquish now the strongholds of the past.

For just once around, I'm told,
We pass through life before we're old.
And to come back through—
We'll never have the chance.

And so to laugh and cry, to hold
All those we love, is more than gold.
To be moved and held—
Yes, caught up in the dance!

I remember, "Seize the day!"
From some movie, show or play
Of a society of poets, dead and gone.

But such impression did it make—
How my attention it did take
To inspire me daily, fill me with song!

And so, daily, will I sing
Of the joy life can bring.
I will seize all that is precious—

All of mine!

I will not come through here again.
You are a love of mine, my friend.
I want to have and hold and love you
While I've time.

Just Emotion

You say I'm just emotional,
a creature of emotion.
My poetry, of the wind
Parodies the ocean.

You say I'm writing far too much
of one peculiar notion.
One gentle breeze, one tender touch
can put my pen in motion.

An Island in My Mind

"You know it's dangerous," he said,
"I could fall easily for you.
I ask of you, please wait for me.
I know it's hard to do."

"But if you go, what will I do?
The wish, the dream will die.
Although you may not understand,
I ask of you, please try."

Yes, let your thoughts remain with me
And if, in fact, we find
We can never be together,
There's an island in my mind.

There we can escape to laugh and cry,
All alone, just you and I.
I'll watch you as you fall asleep
And sing to you my lullaby.

And so my love, do not despair.
I love you so. Please know I care.
Just close your eyes and dream and you will find
You can always have an island in your mind

Someday . . . Some way
Somewhere . . . Somehow.
Not there . . . Not here
Not then . . . Not now

But always and forever you will find . . .
I will love you
On that island
In my mind.

Illusion

You float in—
Like an ethereal god.

Heads turn, nod, and bow.
You glow.

You float in like an ethereal god.
At least . . . it seemed so.

Introspective

Introspective.
Reflective.
My thoughts are all subjective.

Gathering a harvest for the storm.
Will it be enough to keep me warm?

When I've thought it all out, am I spent? Or is there doubt?
And do I have it figured out?

Questions—how I riddle you.
Never meaning to belittle you,
But no real answer have you given me.

If I'm only introspective
I shall see—all the answers
Are in front of me.

Introspective.
Reflective.
My thoughts are all subjective.

Bees that are swarming in my brain,
Searching for a nesting to sustain.

Why can't I conform to what most say
Is "the norm",
And accept all that I see for what it is?

I can't! For I am too inquisitive.

So may I ask, what is the norm?
And tell me why must I conform?
For, to follow suite would be a bore.

So let me question, let me ask.
Perhaps some answers I'll amass.
For the average and the mundane I abhor.

His Slumber

My recitation
Of profound meaning—

I look over. You are dreaming!
Raspy reasoning—You snored.

Could it just be
You're tired and bored?

If

If it proves to be too much—
If it is the thought of my touch
You are evading,

If the feeling is persistent
And pervading—
Oh so chilling!

You might find my touch
Still thrilling,
If it proves to be too much.

If my absence in the summer
Echoes as the season's thunder
If the skies, with wonder,
Open up and rain—
It will be in empathy,
They feel your pain.

If the fields are bare and yearning,
Arid, vulnerable to burning—
Burning with an all consuming,
Hungry fire—
Don't you know?
They are just mocking your desire?

Don't you know?
I have a love for hire—
If it proves to be too much.

Gravity

Gravity, pulling me down.
Can I blame gravity for my frown?
Or should I paint a smile on my face
And dress in the suit of a clown?

For all they really want to see
Is that I appear to be happy.

Inspiration

A contemporary clipping
One, poignant and gripping
I place it again on the shelf.

Tho' often drawn to it
Ne'er do I pursue it
A reminder—much of my own self.

But myself harming
Raw talent disarming
The putting away of the pen.

A deaf ear not listening
Though inside voices, whispering,
"We may not come here again."

Voices are beckoning
Reckless and reckoning
Restless within the soul.

Take thy pen up again
Tell thy stories of then
Rare and rich are the gifts of thy role.

Freedom

Slowly but surely
I feel freedom
from my pain.

A ray of light—
the dawn of time
and no more is the rain.

Funny how freedom
Can light up the world
and make Life feel all the more sane.

Extremes

When I've pushed to the limit—
Extremes—
Seams bursting!

When my head yields to pressure
And my tongue to cursing,
Lines drawn in stressing,
Lips tight in pursing,
It seems to be but a nightmarish dream.
Why can't I see how I go to extremes?

My head is reeling!
Strings drawn tight.
Life, seen as a perpetual fight—
A scream, perhaps,
But I keep it inside.
I feel I am trapped.

Is there room to hide
How I go to extremes?

Forgiveness

When forgiveness
Comes
As an outpouring

Our lives seem no longer
Futile.
Our spirits soar
Beyond boundaries
And meet outside regret.

Yet in forgiveness
We do not forget.

Don't Dare Say You Care

Should I abstain to sustain,
Refrain to regain
my sense of worthiness?

Must I erase your face
From my space,
to replace it with Emptiness?

Or shall I forgive
And live a positive existence?
Relative to what?

To initiate, motivate,
To emulate the greatness
I once sought?

I believe we receive,
Truly achieve
If we conceive it on our own.

So don't even try to deny
That I'll get by
Because I won't be all alone.

Don't even dare say you care
To just ensnare my heart

For I am on my own.

I am free to be me—
And life is easy!
Like a free bird I have flown.

Doubt

A humble beginning—
Underpinned by doubt.

How hard it is to root out!

Experience

Experience—
Like time—
A healer in its own way.

Put on your lipstick
And concealer
To shade the light of day.

Straight ahead—
Surefooted—
Careful not to sway.

Experience—
Like time—a teacher.
Wonder what I'll learn today?

A Step at a Time

I will run—take the ground
Piece by piece under my feet.
I will run strong, steady, stable—
Headstrong and able.

The air, warm,
Melts the remains—
The rubble and ruins the storm has left.
Houses now just a cleft above the ground.

The earth is muddy and brown.
But I choose the concrete,
And run
Until no longer able.

One box of donated toys,
A makeshift table,
A tent to now call home.
All of it blown away

Over night,
Into the wind,
All that I deem to have been rightly mine;
All that I have been—

Or is it?
Maybe now
I am forced to witness
The bareness of my soul—

The most vulnerable part of myself—
Uncovered by possession.
Is my measure earthly treasure,
Or my heart?

All that is left—
What once was a house, now a cleft above the ground.
Yet it's all I have—
Or is it?

I have the sun, the earth, the concrete;
I have two steady feet, moving ahead a step at a time.
I have another day for the sun to shine
And I'll take it a step at a time.

A Pivotal Point

Coming of age—
Growing out it.

Turning each page . . .
Never doubting it.

A pivotal point
In my history

Seeing no further point
In my misery.

A Tree before a Fall

If I lend my ear
to hear you—
Words that sear are mine.
I fear you.

Let shadows creep—
The darkness, deep,
Shall hide my eyes.
For in vulnerability
My peril lies.

For your rising up
To strike me
Travels deep into
My psyche.

And this fear—
As a lion stalks its prey—
Leaves me mute,
Without a single word to say
In my defense.
I shudder—
Guarded, taut, and tense.

Windblown trees
Throw their shadows on the wall.
And I tremble,
As a tree before a fall.

For Your Recovery

The breath of life, a flower,
Yielding beauty by the hour,
Bloom by bloom.

May God grant you
Power
To feel better
              Soon.

An Altered State of Mind

If I could shut it all out, I might.
But then, would that make it all right?
Differing thoughts like day and night—
What would I think? What would I write?

Why must I live to be afraid?
Wondering why. What if I stayed?
Now I'm wishing all my thoughts would cease—
I'm looking for a life of peace.

If I should awake one day to find
An altered sort of state of mind
Or if nothing should exist but a vacuum
Then, I'm realizing, I've room!

These ideas filling me
Are beckoning dreams, possibilities!
Perhaps from these dreams I'd write
(Though such writings peculiar be—

Not quite the same as they used to be)
This time these dreams are right for me.
Peculiar as they may seem or be
My mind, unshackled, is now free.

Out of all in this world I run from

You, my one particular someone,
Affect me most.
Surrealistic apparition, a ghost.

I, from you, my lover, have fled,
To find I've only run away in my head—
To awake and find, I'm not at peace.
My soul is searching for peace.

But serenity I cannot find
For now I've an altered state of mind.
To any solution I am blind,
Living in an altered state of mind.

If I should take refuge in a hidden hill
Would thoughts of you follow me still?
Could I my constitution restore?
Or would your absence only beckon me more?
I'm looking at your photograph.
It's only just your photograph.
Ain't it funny how time passes us by
Runnin' us, tellin' us lies

That forever was for all time—
But never was yours or mine.
And now I awake to find
Forever is an altered state of mind.

A Window in My Mind

I will make for you a window in my mind.
You can raise it when the sun decides to shine,
And close it against the cold and wind.
You can look out, for you are safe within.

It's there I hold you deep within my mind.
I am waiting for the good and perfect time to bring you out—
on a day when I've no doubt.

And you, no more to sit away and pine.
Looking out from behind the window
In my mind.

Be Objective

Don't read your new book
with dirty fingers.
The impression of your mind
will leave marks
on pure white pages,
like prints.

Read it with a clear mind—
intent on learning.
Read it with a clean soul;
a conscience yearning

to be soothed . . .

Read it with hands
that can smooth the pages,
each crease.

Collect your age.
Cease to doubt.
Ease your rage—
But let it out.

Understand you are not the first to feel . . .
You won't be last.
Many in the past have felt the same—
far too many, with worlds far too wide to name.

Know how to collect your time . . .

And linger with an unharnessed soul
over a new page.

But don't read your new book with dirty fingers.

A Woman Now

I'm not free yet—
Not now.
My freedom
Sits on the back burner—
Waiting to be stirred.

A woman now...
I'm lured
By new dimensions,
And demand more from life
Than just attention.

Before

Before
I let your lips
Drive me
To the edges of Ecstasy—

Before
I feel Love's Danger—
Love's Ledges
Beckoning me—

Before
Your eyes draw me in—
Into your Lair of Love,
Your den—

I will recall
All
The Thrill
I am feeling.

I will recall
The Wheel of Lust
Reeling
in my head.

I will look closer
At the Snake
With which I am dealing—
the adder's head

And I Will
Strike it
'Til it is stricken—
Dead.

Absentia

Love in absentia—
Unfulfilling.
Winter's gift—
Bitter chilling.

In my mind
I dare to find
Walls, bare,
Walls lined with absentia.

The Blessing

What Piece can you lift
From your wreckage?
What tenuous metal of scrap?
Can you strip your soul
For a message?
How is your varnish a Trap?

In what way—
To form it and mold it?
Would you hold it again
To your heart?
Is there one who would
Comfort and hold it
When you feel yourself coming apart?

Does your soul dare fathom a start?
With this piece, sparse,
This parcel and part
You once knew of
Your soul and your heart

This piece you lift from wreckage.
Can your soul be prepared for
The message?

A Blessing In Disguise

What piece can you lift
From your wreckage?
What tenuous metal of scrap?
Of poetry—Broken—Unspoken—
Parcel—
Or token mishap?

What piece can you lift
from your wreckage?

What hands move to form it
Or warm it?
What Spirit has spoken
Or seen
How tragedy chose to deform it?
The heart—
Bitter part of the scheme.

How then does the mind
Chance Perceive it?
Is there courage enough
To believe
In the Dream—Enough—
To achieve it
And to learn to Accept
And Receive

The Blessing we find
In our wreckage.

. . . What piece can you lift from your wreckage?

Admittance: A Dawning

To admit one is weak
Does not mean
One seeks opinions.

In a dominion of dreams
It seems
I am drifting.

But speaking my mind
I find
Peace.

A cessation of longing
A sense of belonging
A dawning of peace.

Broken Memory

I see a field of lovely lilies—
Each one a perfect memory.
To what extent can I serve
Each perfect memory, to preserve?

What about the memories I've found—
Worn and broken lilies, faded brown?
If I could only life into thee breathe.
Lost forever, broken memory.

Perhaps, like a message bottle into the ocean tossed,
One memory, perhaps, forever lost—
Lost and lonely bottle out at sea,
Lost forever, lonely memory.

But if our paths by chance should cross—
Waves upon the shore the bottle to toss!
Jostled for a moment, it is true—
I'm stunned at the mere memory of you!

For how is it my mind could let
Such a beautiful memory to forget?
Of all I comprehend and all I see
None of the fair lilies are, to me,

likened to your beauty. Yet I've found
all your fair lilies faded brown!
And, for your memory, no bottle tossed
Upon your shore, my love, for it is lost.

Lost forever bottle out at sea,
Lost forever, broken memory.

A Cup of Poetry

A superfluous, incandescent
Cup of poetry
Like endless nights of endless lights
It flows from within me.

While in the day the words I say
All sound unseemingly—
Within my mind there lies a rhyme
Of serendipity!

Creator of My Doom

Sitting in this dark and empty
Corner of my room.
Where I remain hidden,
The creator of my doom.

Why must I be ridden
With such fear, perennial gloom?
A pariah, downcast;
A societal outcast.

Don't you get too close
For that is what I fear most.
Keep the light out of my eyes—
For light and knowledge, I despise.

Another way I'll never choose—
For to win, to me, is to lose.
I'll remain here in this cell,
The creator of my own hell . . .

Locked away, here, in this room—
The creator of my doom.

I'll wait

I'll wait . . .
Feels my life is but a slate
Without writing

And nothing seems inviting
At the time—
Like life without poetry or rhyme.

But I'll wait—
To anticipate a true love,
A true feeling . . .

To give my heart
Time
It needs for healing.

Denial

You carry it with you—
Like some loss;
A sore, hidden beneath a sleeve.

A blotting out at all costs;
A hand covers the mouth that grieves.
You carry it with you.

You deny
The tears you cry
As if they are not falling.

A blotting out—
the midnight sky
in darkness finds you crawling.

Though you push it far away
The pain,
in reappearing

Reveals itself—
An inner wound
The flesh itself is tearing.

You carry it with you—
Like some loss;
A sore hidden beneath a sleeve.

The stifled cry—

You well disguise
The pain that never leaves.

You carry it with you.

Fragments

If I think of it too hard
I find my mind to be
Broken shards,

Bits of broken pieces,
Broken glass.

Better off to leave behind the past!

Leave it.
Only a true love can grieve it,
Snuff it out.

A gentle hand . . .
You understand without a doubt
My broken pieces, broken shards.

In the Rain

You come to me—
An outstretched hand,
Not as with a coffer
But as one with much to offer,

Bearing fruit!
Shedding light
On the bareness of my branches—
Dry and unyielding;

Saying your harvest will suffice
For mine—
That your grapes
Make the sweetest cherry wine.

But not so soon!
The sun is quite positioned now—
It's noon, and I am dry.
For the rain once again has passed me by

Or rather, is withholding
For that perfect time,
Clouds unfolding
To shed its precious droplets upon me,

To the outstretched branches of my tree,
As for now, I am waiting.
As the clouds from me, abating,
As the wind beats my brittle branches dry.

Though your fruit is ripe and tender,
It pains to be without my splendor
But thirst does not rob me of my lust!
... In the rain once again I'll put my trust.

Focus!

Focus!
Clean the lens.
See what of life you are missing.

Is it whizzing by you?
Don't let life try you—
Try it!

Find a perfect fit,
A perfect glass
That reflects

The present...
Detects the future,
And protects the past.

I Will Not

Unsure of everything;
Uncertain of myself!
Unaware of why my life
Resides on a shelf
With dust covered over,
Yet to be uncovered.
A tender, fragile four-leaf clover
Yet to be discovered!

Selected aventurine
Arranged in such a way
Inconspicuous to the prying eyes.
I must not be displayed.

Chosen with austerity
Upon my silver shelf
Are others that accompany me,
That complement myself.

Seems to be a costly price—
The whisperings and stares—
For entertaining foolishly
And choosing without care
The Dickonsonian 'plated wares'
Upon my silver shelf.
I will not drop in low regard
Pertaining to myself.

Face to Face

We shared before we shared.
We cared before we cared,
And fate somehow found a way to place
You and me together, face to face.

We knew exactly what we wanted.
Circumstance left us undaunted.
No reason to create an alibi.
And time stood still within your eyes.

Fear and Darkness

It's dark.
No room to move—
No room to breathe.

Darkness so dark
Your mind cannot conceive
Which way to turn.

Fear is the fire
Within the mind
Which burns it dry.

Doubt—
The reason I will freeze
And question, "Why?"

"What is it all about?"
Fear and darkness—
Fear and doubt.

No room to move;
No where to turn.
Fear—the fire within my mind

        Burns it dry.

While time and love passes me by.
Still I find I question, "Why?"
What is it all about?

Yet it is love I do without.
Fear and darkness—
Fear and doubt.

Exposure

You give yourself away
in your wondering and ruminating.

There lies no mystery in expatiating your thoughts.

To keep it quiet, you ought—
Tucked away in a velvet-lined box,
Hinge secured, carefully locked.

Keeping those who would invade, at bay.

You know you should,
If only you could.
But you give yourself away.

Mystery of Me

You'll never unlock
The mystery of me.
Too many mysteries
Not enough keys
That fit!

With the combination . . .
The same,
Just when you have
The numbers,
They change

Out of sequence
Lost again
As one probing in the dark
You're hoping for a spark
To light a flame

But you really know
No more
Than my name
And soon you'll surrender
For surely you'll see
You're just an offender

I'm tender and free
And you'll never unlock
the mystery of me.

On Order

My life is clearly
Ordered
At times, it
Borders
On insanity
While my vanity
Which clips me in two
Leaves me halved
In the center
With nothing
To chew.

No Longer

I consider you to exist as a voice, not heard,
A name, not spoken.

There is, no more, a token of my grief,
For at present, my heart has found relief.

I sense your name, but my pen does not write it.
To hear it, is not the same, for my heart does not delight in it

Any longer.

I stand stedfast, stronger on my view—
For my heart no longer yearns for you.

I know you no more to be

        An invasion of my privacy—
        An intrusion on my senses.

Not because I am full of denial
Or pretenses—

But facing the truth;
And no longer a victim of my youth.

I stand stedfast, stronger on my view—
For my heart no longer yearns for you.

No More

You were in love,
    My turtledove.
You deemed my love befitting
All your charms
And "up in arms"
But now it seems you're quitting.

No Chance

A pensive glance—
Though there's no chance I'll enlist you
As a possible recipient of my love.

A hesitant hand
Above the paper that denies your name,
The one my mind is thinking of.

A message in each song
Although it is wrong to think of you,
It's hard not to, I'll admit.

A tingling in the air—
Though I do not dare feel it.
A silence in the night—
It isn't right how you steal it.

You have your way.
How you play on my mind.
And it's real, so real.

But I'll never enlist you as a possible recipient
Of my love.

Will I?

Will I cease to grow in your shadow?
Crouched in solitude
Where no light can get to me,
Can I command attention
If you are all they see?

Will I cease to grow in your shadow?

My Destiny

Happiness, come find me!
I will view each challenge kindly.
Of these three, please follow me:
Peace, joy, and prosperity.

In my life, let love surround me!
For my destiny has found me.
I accept all that is lost
For these are necessary costs.

To stray, I will not from this path
Though it appears it has
Many turns, and twists, and trails—
I will continue, and prevail.

No other path shall ensnare
Down no other path I'll dare
For there is no other way!
So for faith and strength, I'll pray.

Weather, not always so fair,
Though it may seem sunshine is rare,
In the end I've found
Peace and happiness abound.

And my direction, my way
Seems to grow clearer every day.
Peace and joy, prosperity
Are walking hand in hand with me.

Pray and Fight

Pray and fight.
Fight and pray.
Thank God for another day.

    Pray.

Fight and pray.
Pray and fight.
Thank God for the lonely night.

    Fight.

Do You

Do you dare come to me
When fear cramps the love
You are extending?
When my depression threatens all
We hold dear?

Do you dare—
When my only thought is
Of an ending,
To care enough to
Find me here?

Where my sorrows leave
A broken fallen form
Upon the floor,
Do you dare offer solace?
Do you dare love me
More?

I *Picture* It

I'd like to gambol through my days
Through open fields, newly shorn;
To awaken with a seraphic smile
On one peculiar morn
Take this big world by the tail
And wrap it all around me!
All cares into the wind I'd flail
And, from the biggest tree—
The biggest, tallest tree I'd find,
I'd climb into a cloud!
Spread far and wide my narrow grasp
And with a voice so loud
I would serenade the angels
And make the heavens ring!
My voice would echo lovelier
Than all the cherubs sing.
I picture it, I see myself
As no one else has done.
Of all God's children in the world
Alone, to be the one
To break the stony barrier;
To live, breathe, love, care,
I'll take my chance and dare
To shine as brightly as the sun.

Food for Thought

While you collect
Food for thought
Somewhere
Another starves,

Marred by the negligence
Of your hands—
Scarred by the reticence,
Your resistance.

Strands of hope
Rendered hopeless
By your devotion
To other plans.

A Noble Prize

Why is it I hesitate?
Why must I wait?
Or feel a certain sign must come along
to seal my fate?

Deep within your eyes—
Within them lies a certainty.
You hold me as a noble prize
And there you wait for me.

There, in your corner of the world,
I hear your destined pleas.
The feeling, clear, you want me near
where love is soft and free—

Where love is carefree as the wind,
Uncomplicated, yet,
Where you and I remain as friends
As we were when we met.

So many times to ponder—
Where did this love come from?
Should I hold to it tightly
Or turn from it and run?

Where, then, would my love hide?
For still a love would live inside.
One day to see, love ne'er did flee
For our love, still, resides.

Does not forget a whisper
Does not forget a glance.
Our love won't forget the day
We took our fated chance

And crossed the line where we now find
a passion runs so deep.
A treasure found, our love abounds,
a love worthy, to keep.

Our Choice

Interwoven as a thread,
Words, chosen to be said.
Life, a cloth we spread—
the pattern is our choice.

Life—a work of art.
Choose your script and play your part
Fill it with your mind and heart
Draw from your inner force!

Decorate life how you may.
Choose your color. Choose your way.
Choose the perfect chords to play
Then Lift your mighty voice!

I Learned

I learned love
Had nothing to do with looks,
Or Love in the crook of my finger
Or a picture perfect man,
A dead ringer!
Understand?

I learned love
Is a spasm of the heart,
An upstart of emotion,
A synergistic explosion,
An unexpected twist!
A love felt such as this—
A real stinger!

You showed me love
Worth bowing down to,
Forsaking all to pursue—
Making such a "to do"!
A "gotta have you" kinda love!
Love that lingers.

You showed me love
Barring nothing . . .
Love for the loving.
Unconditional,
Untraditional,
But love nonetheless.

Love. Then, I guess it is love.

Perspective

Today, I am old.
My face has told a thousand
    Earthly stories.
With pride I've felt a carnal,
    Fleshly glory—
Of Beauty, like a flag unfurled
Ranking me, in my own little world
    To be someone
Worth a second glance
    Someone
With a second chance at life!

    . . . Someone more than just your wife.

But I lay my older hand, bemused, upon your leg.
Thinking of our frivolous trials,
    I smile.

Wouldn't Blame You

Wouldn't blame you
If
You walked away.

Not too much to say
That hasn't been said.
Far too much spinning in my head . . .
Far too much dread.

How close we've come
To moving on,
And yet, I sit here,
All alone.

Not much left now . . .
Less to say.
So I wouldn't blame you if
You walked away.

Nights full of controversy,
Back and forth,
Debating.

It's so very hard for me.
All the time,
Hating to let go.

I feel for you.
I think you know—
It cannot last.

Still, you wait for it to pass you by.
No strength to try . . .
Love, I'll just deny.

Feeling it slip away—
What a price to pay to open up your heart.
But you knew it from the start.

Not much left now . . .
Less to say.
So I wouldn't blame you if
You walked away.

A Star

There is a grace with which you are.
You reside in my life
As a star

That can't be fixed—
Caught between night and day
And everything you say

Seems to draw attention.
Just the mere mention of you
Leaves me with few alternatives.

Just a desire to live and pursue
All I can possibly have
With you.

Letting Go

I am letting go
And now, somehow,
I think you know.

I used to hold you in my heart
Thinking I could be part
Of everything you do.

Believe enough, it will come true.

I thought, to hold you in my mind
For a long and steady time,
That soon enough you would be mine.

But now, I'm letting go.
Somehow, I think you know.

See, life is too short for me to resort
To this make believe.

How could you lie
And not realize, I know,
I've been deceived?

For I've been around.
I know the sound of silence, here.
No one is there.

There is no one to care

For my hopes and fears.
So I'm letting go.

Somehow I think you know.
You sense it within.
You know, this way, I win.

I'm beginning again—
In this letting go.
You, the loser, know.

I'm letting go.

Mercy

To take comfort in the
Inordinate goodness of others

Is to realize the gaggle of sin
this mercy covers.

Movin' Along

Movin' along in society.
Breakin' these ties that are binding me.
Movin' along.

Livin' my life
With my own sense
Of grace.

Life I have known
At my own sense
Of pace.

No haste.
No waste.
Movin' along.
Just movin' along.

Singin' this song
'bout my own sense of glory.
Singin' this song
Tellin' my story.

With good taste
At my own pace.
Movin' along.
Movin' along.

Without You

There in the darkness
You find my spirit,
Torn.

Even in the black of night
You sense it
That I mourn.

No sound I make—
No evidence
Of how my soul is worn

Eyes cast down
A joy removed—
A soul that is forlorn

Give me back my spirit!
You seized it
Now you hear it

Crying out.
Silently
I shout.

Achingly,
I do without
You.

Loneliness

Loneliness
Fills me up
Like a chasm,
An abyss

Stretching
    Yearning
        Longing
            Crying

Worry
    Hurt
        Fear
            of dying.

Loneliness
Fills me up
With nothing.

A Diversion

Has life become
A new dress?
A lipstick shade?
How many times
To be made over
Before you lose
Who you are?

How many paths
To follow
And, pray tell,
Just how far
Will you divert
For a diversion

Before Life—
Convergent
And converging
Upon itself—
Leaves you
A useless heap

Two feet tall
And three feet deep
In the mess
With nothing
But a new lipstick shade
And a new dress.

Not the Average Kind

Why must I do without you, day after torpid day?
When I could take you right along—I know I'll find a way!
If I could shrink you to a size and put you in my purse—
I'd make my preparations and checking on you, first,

I'd be sure of the compartment. Are you a comfortable fit?
Do you have room to move about—to stand and lie and sit?
Could you make the journey, as fitting as a seam?
Stay quietly within my purse until I deem

Appropriate to bring you out—and now the hardest part—
Return you to normal size. Magic, indeed an art
Undiscovered by most of normal, average minds.
But you and I both know that we are not the average kind.

We'd shrink, inflate—we'd bend or stretch
To make it all work out.
There's nothing we find too far-fetched.
That's what our love's about.

Ponderance

Herein lies the rot...

That I should be seeking
What I've already got.

Real Joy

In what way could express
The joy you've given me?
I could scan the alphabet
Complete from A to Z

To find the perfect letters
To create the perfect words—
To convey in such a perfect way
The things you've never heard.

But would this make a difference?
Would my efforts be in vain?
For there's no way to describe such joy
And no way to explain

All this happiness inside—
From all this joy I cannot hide!
But to let you know it's you I love
And in you I confide.

A full life—
Complete and never ending
My spirit knows no limit
To the joy you are sending.

Real joy—
That's what you bring me
Each and every single day
My heart is joyously singing.

And I suppose
This will, alone, suffice
To call it real joy—
To say it's really nice.

Premonition

There exists a love
So deep
You can feel its hurt
Before
It is affected.

Such a love,
So bittersweet—
You will deem it
Worth
Keeping your heart protected.

Rain Song

Rain, Rain,
Falling from the sky.
The feeling is like teardrops
Falling from my eyes.

To form a river of tears
From all my fears
Would drain my spirit dry.

I fill my cup.
I lift it up
To the Lord on high.

Bless me now, I am asking.
Pour your blessing out on me.
Fill my cup. I lift it up.
I give all to thee.

You mark my path.
All I ask is that you send to me
Strength from above—undying love—
Rain pouring down on me.

Resolve

To make a difference in my life—
I must.
I long to lean,
To learn to trust
In you;
Show me how to.

For life is full of peril in pursuit.
And apathy a sterile substitute.

Remnants

Bottle of wine—
At least, what is left.
Vision in my mind—
How you looked . . .

How I felt

Leaves me to no conclusion.
Only leaves me in confusion.
Leaving me to feel bereft,
While I wonder . . . what is left?

Missing you I see
I'm missing part of me.
And what about my heart
For you have torn it all apart.
Did you think you could just take it?
Or did you decide to break it?

Now that you have left
I've noticed quite a cleft—
A division, a split,
And a feeling this is it.
Leaving me to feel bereft
While I wonder . . .

What is left?

Validation

I am happy
Because
I am free.

I am free
Because
I am happy
To be me.

Vain Whisperings

Vain whisperings . . .
An inconspicuous attack!
Who is listening
While you talk behind my back?

Don't say I'm paranoid,
When it's the truth you avoid.
These slanderous words you afford
Cut me like a sharpened sword.

Vain Whisperings . . .
An inconspicuous attack!
Have another cover while
You stab me in the back.

My little man can hear
As you are whispering in his ear.
What is that I hear you say?
Can I come out with you and play?

You lie in wait to entrap me!
Why must success imprison me?
No grist I give you for the mill,
And yet, you want to grind it, still.

One dreaded day, one traitor's kiss
Put Christ on Calvary's hill.
Nails driven through his hands,
And thorns upon his head.

Although you know he lives today
You'd rather he be dead.

Jealousy, it's all the same.
Vain whisperings, a lowly game!
No grist I give you for the mill—
And yet you want to grind it still.

"Vengeance is mine", said the Lord,
"And I will repay."
Each vain and foolish whispering
He hears every day

He judges. He will discern
Who must be denied and spurned.
Remember, as you're whispering,
On his throne, He's listening.

My little man can also hear,
As you are whispering in his ear.
No grist I give you for the mill,
And yet, you want to grind it

        Still.

Resistance

A contemporary clipping
One, poignant and gripping.
I place it again on the shelf.

Though often drawn to it
Ne'er do I pursue it.
A reminder much of own self.

But, myself harming
Raw talent disarming,
Putting away the pen.

A deaf ear not listening
'Though inside, voices whispering,
"We may not come here again."

Voices are beckoning,
Reckless and reckoning,
Restless within the soul.

Take up your pen again
Tell your stories of then
Rare and rich are the gifts of your role.

Peaceful Pathways

Love, Your release . . .
Let it flow.
It's a peace
You will know

In your heart—
In each vein!
Every part of your brain
It will fill!

As it lifts and sustains—
Be
Comfortably still.

Here's a key to my mind
And if you find the time—
Come in.

Walk peaceful pathways
Where you've been.
If you like, you can stay—

For more than a day and a half!
It is yours to decide—
There is no need to ask.

Come and go as you please.
Here you can be.
Here you can breathe.

For it must seem familiar to you . . .
The air is warm
The skies blue and clear.

There is always something new
And I am always here
For you

These pathways that wind—
These trails in my mind—
They've all seen you before.

So many times you've come
Through my door—
Even before I gave you the key!
For in reality
How easily you'd step in
Had you been in my mind
All the while, all the time?

Every turn, twist, and trail
You follow
So well

And they welcome you
Each turn, each pathway
They welcome you.
If you like, please stay.

Poetic Ways

I spend most my days
Picking flowers
Anthology—
Weeding for hours.

In my search for each book
I realize it took
Patience—
Of infinite power

Each one
With its own eerie quality—
Full of words,
So resonant, rare.

Demeanor admired
Indefatigably
I find my felicity there!

Hour and hours
And days on end
I find I am dazzled
And dazed!

Indisposed
As to how and why
And baffled
By poetic ways!

Poetic Ways 2

I spend most my days
Drawing flowers;
Another color;
Another hour.

Prisms of words
Countries of which
You've never heard
To move and to stir

Your imagination—
Inanimate objects
That talk and fill you
With fascination

And wonder!
It's an emotional spell
You're under!
Sensational

Pictures of thunder
Lightning and rain.
Poetic pictures of pain.

It's not just
What you say
But how it is said
And the poetic way it is read

Can breathe life
Into the quiet
And the dead.

Poetry Man

Where are you now,
My poetry man?
You don't write the rhythm,
But I can.

For it is true
That my mind is anew
Is fresh with emotion
With one look at you.

What's up
My poetry man?
The one—did I mention—
Who holds my attention?

What new story to tell you,
Oh poetry man?
To move you so much,
To seduce your touch

Oh poetry man,
My poetry man.

Poetry

Feel the heat clog your pores—
Mere memories in repression;
Horrors the mind stores—
They call it suppression.
But poetry gives horror

    True expression.

A voice: to grieve.
A laugh: to relieve.
An ancient eclectic
Effective reprieve:

    Poetry.

A brush with which to draw
Love, unaffected, in the raw;
A tear I thought I saw:

    Poetry.

That with which to leave a mark;
Perhaps a hatred, cold and stark;
Perhaps a flicker in the darkness
Of one's mind.

Stored away like seasoned wine—

Poetry.

My poetry.

Riddance

Guilt, a feeling I choose to package into kindling paper.
I am burning it up!
There are tiny, nearly invisible ashes that remain.
I watch them as they scatter and disappear into the wind,
never to be seen or felt again.

Portrait

It's twenty 'til three
And it's getting to be too much.

It's twenty 'til three—
Where's the hand I can
Reach out and touch?

Pull me up! Calm me.
Set me free from this panic!
I know how my body plays tricks on my mind.

It feels blurry and blinding—
A compulsion!
I feel compelled!

But I remember how you held me
In my times of need
Your voice is soothing.

I hear you plead,
"Don't do it.
I'll help you through it."

It's twenty 'til three . . .

Hold my hand.

Real Living

Real living is . . .
    A heartbeat . . .
    Due in one week . . .
    The pitter-patter of little feet!

A smile so sweet . . .
    He looks-
    like me!
    Now my living is complete.

The Confines

I live within the confines
Of my money
And there's always someone
Pursuing me
Wanting a little bit.
But before they're finished-
They've taken all of it!
Then I'm through!

Another creditor to answer to—
I've got a job to do!

I live within the confines of my money!

It seems a never-ending process
This day-in, day-out
Struggle to progress
What's it all about?

I can't seem to even make a dent
It's time to pay the rent—Again!
I just can't seem to win!

I live within the confines of my money

I've never been one of the
"Upper-crust"
But still, if "looks can kill"
My budget will die

Always something new to try
"Buy or bust to be one of us "
In God we trust—
I pray he'll slay my wonderlust!

I live within the confines of my money.

Resentment

A lull in the conversation,
    felt in the air as
        constant stress.

Silence. Hesitation
    comes from having nothing
        to address

to compliment.

It is this silence I resent.

Feelings contradict, conflict, and mesh . . .

And I wear them as a wound upon my flesh.

The Culminating Point

He tried to correct my cry,
In vain to refurbish my eye
To see the reasons,
The "why" of my existence.

Plainly he did stay
With a love I'll ne'er repay.
For what am I to say
To such persistence?

Herein have I clung to dreams
It seems I've hung
On the ladder, the middle rung
Of my ascendance.

Ascending to new heights
I keep my dreams within my sight.
The dreams enable me to fight
For my resplendence.

Beauty, to the eye,
Is blessed upon me
As I try to reach high, ever higher
In my attendance to my goal.

My simple, most difficult goal,
To refurbish all my soul
To find a oneness, find a wholeness
In self-acceptance.

I lift my dreams from off the rung—
A sweeter, stronger song I've sung
And an endless love I've won
Without resistance.

The Living

You say
"It's personal".
It's true—
Concealed in a drawer
For a season

With an untold rhyme
And a reason
Not given,
Except for living a life
That is joined
With the living.

The Only Key

I continue into the night, my spirit, drained.
But thoughts of you beset me,
Creep around inside my brain.

How do I handle it, release it, let it out?
Do I exorcise it?
Do I hunger, scream or shout?

From the depths of my soul
I feel you speak to me!
You tell me you are caged
And that I hold the only key.

"Set me free!" I hear you calling.
"From this prison set me free!"
My only wish, to be with you
To hold you close to me.

But I keep you locked away inside
Like feelings that I choose to hide.
A matter of my foolish pride
That I should choose to put aside

All the things you mean to me
and everything that we could be.
You are repressed. You are not free.
And I hold the only key.

Waiting

On days like this I feel my load
Is lighter.
Amazing, this, as if my soul
Is quieter—
Pain abating.

My very self, resisting,
And waiting
For words to come,
Overtake—
Then run.

You Can

You have my permission
    Oh beautiful man
        To love me forever...
            As long as you can.

You Get Me High

Do you know you are the one?
You are my dawn, my setting sun.
You are my reason to begin.
You are the fire that burns within!

You get me high!
Yes you, you set my soul afire.
I can't deny—
You are the one that I desire.

In you I've found a resting place.
With you all obstacles I face.
And I conquer with a smile
For you're beside me all the while.

It's you, you put my mind at ease.
You are the one I want to please.
Another love I'll never try.
You lift me up, you get me high.

It's you, you put my mind at ease.
You are the one I want to please.
Another love I'll never try.
You lift me up. You get me high.

You get me high!
Yes you, you set my soul afire!
I can't deny
You are the one that I desire.

Another love I've never known
With all the tenderness you've shown.
It's you I want to be around
For all the happiness I've found

Now the future I see clearly
For to have and hold you near me
Is my reason to begin.
I feel the fire that burns within.

You get me high!
High as the highest mountaintop
This feeling's right
And it's never gonna stop.

The Young Heart

A young heart—
Torn,
Tearing.
Lips parted,
Swearing love poems on the breeze.

Hands
Smearing feelings on my sleeve,
Feelings felt in that young heart.

A breast
Full of burden—
Oh who's to say the children cannot love?
For love is free.
And they can love
Like you and me.

Oh the young heart!

The Written Word

I have not yet begun to fight,
To use my pen these words to write—
To wield them as a sword—
To move both forward and toward

To unleash with all my might
To unharness in the night
To freely let my feelings go—
To let my inner spirit show.

But then, would they trample me?
Or would my words set me free?
Why should I despise
all those who mock and criticize?

For one voice is one set of eyes.
I will be labeled, listed, sized.
And one voice is one opinion
in one world, in one dominion.

Why should I really care?
For to continue I will dare
To write these words and to be heard,
although I might not be preferred.

Now one opinion is one voice
And everyone will make a choice.
But I will still survive.
And to write these words, I thrive.

Timeless

Timeless,
Surpassing time and man;
My love for you is timeless.
Can you ever understand?

The way I feel about you
Can't be measured.
There's no space
Sufficient, to confine it.

No building, no place
Could house or hold it.
There is no way to control it—
For it fills me up! It fills my very soul!

The very thought of you possesses me—
I am completely whole.
An entire entity—
Complete divinity.

Always and forever
It will last—
After earth and space
And all of time has passed.

So wherever in this world you may go
You can be sure,
I just want you to know
My love for you is timeless.

To Regard Circumstance

A blank stare . . .
A heart that won't care
And mind doesn't dare to invent.

A dream left, not followed.
Hope, swallowed.
A life, hollowed . . .
Unsent.

What is life without dreaming?
Does it not lose its meaning?
Or is the meaning unseemingly
Bent—

Twisted, distorted—
Unclear and contorted;
Like words out of focus,
In print!

When life has no binding
We're learning and finding
We're steadily minding
Our dreams.

Life, our chance to be still
Or to dance!
To regard circumstance
As it seems.

Sea of Me

Always do I want to be around you.
My heart was empty, searching,
and it found you.
My love—let it warm and surround you,
Strengthen and astound you.
A love so wet
I'll drown you
In a sea of me.

The Wine

I have to get away,
To taste the wine again today;
To swirl it slowly on my tongue;
To really hear the song as it is sung.

The dream-
It seems the pressure
Is forever suffocating.

Seems too often now
I'm pondering and waiting to be writing.
While nothing is inviting.

Can you tell?
Remember how my heart would swell
And buckle in the prison of my bones?

A heart that now feels angry and alone
And left behind.
Obligations lend frustrations
To my heart and soul and mind

Life seems yet to send temptations
And though this, the part I find
I am resisting—
It seems I am missing you too often.

So I must say . . .
I desire to taste the wine again today.
Did I tell you? *You* are the wine.

Sent Away

She came to me in the color of her youth
When, flowers sprouting, prudently in her eyes
Detailed all the heavy meanings of her sighs
And sacrament...

How it was she was sent to me
I'll never know enough to tell—
For I never understood—
Sent her away
And wished her well.

Revelation

Salty brine—the taste on which I dine
When my anger—as a lion raucously spent—
Reduces itself shamelessly to tears.

Salty brine—the taste on which I dine
When my anger—cowering in corners—
Translates to fear.

Bitter and scalding, my soup,
As I face the Ruthless Truth
Of my transgressions.

Falling short of my professions,
I stand much smaller than before.
No will have I to crack the door—continue on.

With no progression in the dawn—
The light of day
Is stagnate-finding a shadow in which to play.

On these days when I am crazed with all undone,
Pacing back and forth the earth,
I curse the sun.

But thank you Lord for days of tea,
As sweet as honey from the bee that brings.
I pray you, bee, withhold your sting!

And this honey, sweet, I'll savor

"til I'm done—
Beaming, bursting, smiling at the sun.

For suddenly, in its reflection
I find our love, in its perfection, overdue.
Suddenly revealed to me, my love for you.

Sense of Loss

And what now, for your sense of loss?
How much love did your pride cost?

A quiet home, an empty bed
And all those useless words she said
Drop like copper pennies on the floor.
Dead—for they won't be said anymore.

There was no one to listen at the time
To the message spoken there, within her rhyme.
And necessary discussion—Fell—
Like loud percussion on your ear.

All that you could offer was conversation
Hot enough to sear.

So keep you words unto yourself
Like dusty books upon a shelf.
See how much love your pride can cost
As you survey your sense of loss.

Sunlight

Sunlight, Sunlight
Shining on my senses.
Pure bright white light—
Strengthen my defenses!

To prove all that I am
All that I ever dream to be—
I might use this inner force
To set me free.

Sunlight, Sunlight
Shining on my senses.
Pure bright white light—
Diminish all pretenses!

A light upon the knowledge
In my soul
That o'er my destiny
I only have control.

For I am only part
Of this desire in my heart.
And it's true that even I
If given wings could learn to fly!

My potential knows no limit
Like the sky.
And I am like the sun
For even I

Aspire to be around
To enlighten and astound
To inspire and to touch
To be needed just as much

As the sun that warms my face!
Bring me light and strength and grace!
And a reason to move on
With each new awakening dawn.

Sunlight, Sunlight
Smiling on my senses.
Pure, bright white light—
Cleansing and redemption!

So now I'll take a part
Of this desire in my heart—
Draw from the strength it can impart
And find a place to make a start.

Societal Prejudice

A soul filled with dread;
A life
Severed—
Broken thread.

Life in an incubator;
A ride in an elevator
That has stopped—
Never will reach the top.

They take my joy away-
All those who say
It isn't right . . .
That black doesn't belong with white.

But I love you, anyway.
Let them say what they say
And do as they will do
For my love will be with you.

That Steely Trap

Like a bear loose in the woods
You, my friend, also know you should
Keep your foot clear of that steely vise.

That trap will snare you every time.
These words to you are kind.
Heed these words. Regard this good advice.

Discretion.
Privacy.
No mention or suggestion.

But should you give in to
That steely tongue,
Soon enough you'll find the damage done!

One too many words were said
And one too many heard—
And then it is a mystery to no one

Exactly all that you're about
Now the intrigue is in doubt
You're common knowledge as the day is done.

For your own mouth is your own trap.
Don't put your foot within its grasp
Or you may find it in a steely vise.

Just find something vague to say.
Keep it brief. Be on your way.
Or a swollen foot may be your price.

Something to Gain

Raw honesty
It is fitting.
It unfetters the mind.

All else leaves one
Blind
To the strangeness
Of the mix.

You can
Transpose
Transfix;
Carry your heart
On a crucifix
Or veil it
With a smile.

All the while
Enduring
The pain
And hoping
You've something left
To gain.

Unexpected

I sit down—
Unaware of what I've found.
Ideas surround me
like pieces of puzzle on the ground
scattered

free of form.
Thoughts, not of the norm.
Ideas find me—
An unexpected storm—
Like winter's freeze!

Leaves, shaken from the trees,
These thoughts drift in.
Ideas find me
Like thoughts blown in on the wind,
Ever so gently.

Flowers sent to me
From one I do not know:
Flowers blossoming.
See how they grow free from the vine,

Like these thoughts in my mind.
They unravel, unwind
And fall, free, on the page.
Unaware of time—
Unaware of age—

They are part of myself.
But I put them away,
Far removed, on the shelf.
Words, not dead.
Simply, words I have said.

Unheard

Oh God
I am afraid
But I am yearning.

The solstice
Burning within me
Is a bitter fuse
Of life, extending . . .
Yet I must choose.

The course is lazy,
Open wide—
And I am wrapped up,
Safe inside . . .
Too comfortable for words.
And all mine,
Left,
Unheard.

Upon the Slate

That's how the mind operates—
Like a slate without writing.
Then we begin
Printing with an imaginary pen,
Words and colors—pictures of our own—
Things we've seen
And others, never known.

But if terror grows too full to face—
If we feel it from the horror we trace,
Ideas unproductive, (call it sin),
We can erase the slate.

This time, a rainbow in the sky.
We draw ourselves as if with wings to fly.
For, indeed, we all aspire to rise above—
To spread our wings and fly, as if a dove.

But like a dove we do not fly alone.
So we trace into the scene a love we've known,
And spread our wings together, fly as doves.
For no picture is complete if without love.

That's how the mind operates—
Like a slate without writing,
Then we begin—
Determine with the drawing of our pen
The pictures of our life as it should be.
Our mind has its own eyes with which to see.

ROBYN WALLACE KILPATRICK

Our lives are put in motion as we believe
To bring into fruition what our minds have preconceived.
And no picture too lofty or too great
If we can draw it on our mind—upon the slate.

My Gift

This I can give:
The warmth of my measure,
The fruit of my growth.
This, all I have.
I give this to you; both.

This I can offer:
Freedom unsuppressed,
To create and express;
And always to address your feelings,
that you may grow and prosper.

His Gift

He comforts me with all he has
The glow of a candle, the warmth of desire
In the privacy where he draws my bath
At the end of the day as I lanquish and tire.

And oh, what sensation of luxury—
Fresh linen and quiet and song;
The escape in the sound of his symphony;
The escape in his arms so strong.

Here in the quiet of music and thought,
Nearby the gift of poetry he brought
Lay unopened, untouched, for suddenly, so much,
I'm awaiting the peace I have sought.

Peace, come and fill me. Console me and still me
Like rain when I've nothing to do.
Like new life I'm winning, completely beginning.
Like lovers who'll always be true.

Hands that reach out to comfort me
Trace with fingers the shape of my face.
Eyes caressing me tenderly
Would, if could, all my worries erase.

He comforts me with all he has:
The glow of a candle, the warmth of desire
In the privacy where I, luminous, bask
in the glow of his spirit, the warmth of his fire.

Love Wasted

Love I'll never have—
Love wasted.
Love I've been denied—
Yet, I have tasted.

Why do they say,
"The best in life is free?"
And yet, I cannot have you
Here with me.

To earn your love,
What could I do?
And in what way
Could I pursue moments of ecstasy I treasure?

To share them with you,
Is what I would do.
Time spent—
Time without measure

To do the things I long to do—
To touch, without touching you—
To move you and to fill you
Through and through.

For I can touch without touching,
I can move you with my glance.
You know all this is true, and yet
You'll never take the chance.

It's such a shame to be a dancer,
Yet to never have your dance.
Moreover, likened to a gambler
Who will never have his chance.

It will come and go, your moment,
Your certain time, your circumstance.
Oh what a shame to be a lover
Yet, to never have romance!

Yet you'll blame it on the moment,
The certain time, the circumstance.
You'll say you are not really free.
You'll waste this precious chance.
It's a time to be together,
Yet, too soon it slips away.
Time encroaches on the morrow,
Soon, to be our "yesterday".

Love I'll never have.
Love wasted.
Love I've been denied.
And now, I face it.

Why do they say,
"The best in life is free."
And yet, I cannot have you
Here with me.

Love That Can

You can be in love, and it changes,
Share love with a stranger
You call friend;
See it blossom, grow, change . . .
Feel it end.

Love changes.

Oh to find a love
That I can keep!
Oh to feel it Safe to fall in
Deep—
Up to the neck!

To wreck the nerves!
Take the curve
And complete it.
Confront the hurt
And defeat it.

Love that can stand
Surpass
Look into the past
And appreciate the present
For all it is.

Love that can make the future
      A positive experience.

An existence so profound—
An omnipresence!
Around you I want to be.
Let me be free to love you
'til eternity.

An Undue Chore

The words—
They pour
Like a sore
Whose pus must let

An undue chore
It is
To forget

For in remembering
Is found
Freedom
From regret

An Impregnable Force

You, an impregnable force—
You haunt me, with no remorse!

I, left with no recourse, cannot deny you—
With no method, no recourse by which to get away,
I am resolved, removed in the day.
But somehow, something isn't right.
For now, you haunt me in the night.

You—a seamless form of human nature,
Spiritual incense, a vapor;
A mesmeric lunatic;
An evil, dirty trick.

You inebriate me—
Drunken with your presence,
I, supplanted with your look
Am found, without resistance.

You disguise yourself,
As others I see in my dreams—
People I thought I could trust
But something intangible seems

To give way—perhaps a word or way
They say what they say
Or do what they do.
But, suddenly it's not they, but you!

And I am taken aback
As one under sudden attack!
A fear I feel, unrivaled.
I move to scream, yet I am stifled,

Suffocated, choked.
I try to fight, but
I can't move my arms!
(Is this some sick sort of joke?)

You drain all my will—
Like a sponge.
Into the depths of this water,
I plunge

Hoping, soon I will drown,
Awaken from this nightmare,
Awaken to find
There's no one there!

To awake in a world
Without obsession—
To live in world
Where I am no one's possession,

Controlled by desire;
Where my soul is not afire
With longing and lust,
Where there is trust.

But I have none!
I trust no one!
And your spirit haunts me—
Still—I feel it!

Given Awhile

Your smile
Reminiscent of that which I'm missing.
Bittersweet lips
I am no longer kissing.

Winter leaves that fall—
They once were my shade.
Now they exist,
A cool, glamorous façade—

A coat of color upon the ground
Yet, how soon to lose luster,
Turn brown.

Like your smile,
Everything fades,
Given awhile.

Cynical eyes
See through
Your smile.

Love to you
Is but trust
Put to trial.

True color, turned brown.
An image, fallen down.
Smile, turned to frown—

Given Awhile.

Longing for Home

I want to get home
To my poetry.

Always it seems
I'm on the road,
No one knowing me
But you . . .

I want to get home to you, too.

Had Not Seen You

Had not seen you in a while
My mind had not been haunted
By your smile—
At least, not quite as much

But then I saw you last night
And watched
As you talked to me
And I realized how I hunger for your touch.

Hungry, yet afraid.
What if I stayed with you?
Tell me, if we consummate our love,
Then what would we do?

For my body would never let
My mind be free—
Never able to forget
For one single moment!

Had not seen you in a while.
Now my mind is so haunted
By your smile—
And my body, hungry for your touch.

Maybe this feeling will last
A lifetime—
Even after I'm gone from this earth!
Maybe neither of us will find

Any love of such value or worth.
It makes me sad.
Another life I see painted in your face—
You, that someone I never had.

And though I want you so much
I know I must let it rest
And rejoice in how you've touched my life—
How it has been blessed.

I'll say a prayer for this
My love
Always I wish for you
the best.

Love's Respite

Chewing me up for my faults—
Spitting me out on the asphalt!
Between my own words I am caught!
For a noble reason I have sought—

Still, I search even more as I write
For words that would make it all right.
Why must love, it's own to respite?
Tell me, why must we argue and fight?

Enslaved

Hellfire and Brimstone
Belt buckle and Broomstick
What is the difference?
And who, even of a child,
Can tell?

It began as a disguise,
A discipline,
As an elaborate acknowledgement
Of the hiding of the truth...
The painting of pretty corners

A putting on of theatrical masks,
Each particular one
Intended to convey
What one thought
Another might want to know

To disclose the ugly truth...
Yet volumes of pretty prose
Dainty corners
All begin somehow
To echo the truth

As the carefully chosen mask erodes
Its paint thins, chips,
Even so, and in accordance,
The future is ever enslaved
To always bear out truth.

Transition

My head is interceding
While the pain is faintly pleading,
Pleading, "What about your heart?
How can you fathom now a start,
Without your heart?

While the jonquils blooms are blooming
My heart will overrule,
Is dooming any chance to dance in springtime
With the love that once was mine.

I stand still as light, pervading,
Seems each shadow to be grading
And the darkness now is fading
That once fell upon my heart.

Now I find my movements moving
With the sound of spring,
Now proving in the dawn
That life goes on,
And leaves us separate and apart.

Winds Whisper Your Name

Why is it you affect me
Even when you're not here?
How is it you speak to me
Although you're nowhere near?

How is it that you stay with me
At all times of the day?
Surely others wonder
Why it is I feel this way!

Don't they know how much I love you?
Can't they see it in my eyes?
Or is it our secret?
Are we the only ones alive?

I feel surely we must be—
For you are all I see!
And I would be a rich girl—
A dollar every time you think of me.

Say my name and I'm aware.
Call out loud and I'll be there.
All things remind me of you.
Even winds whisper your name.

A Hard Stance

A hard stance—
This back-stabbing
A clutching and grabbing
At many
Creates lots left
Who don't have any.

Dangerous

I'm kinda dangerous
In your heart

I am dangerous
As the one
Who lights the spark

I'll give you love
Just like a drug—

Then I'll pull the plug

I'm dangerous.

I'm kinda lethal
To your mind
I am the thought you
Always find

I am the knot you
Can't unwind—
The love that makes you blind
I'm dangerous.

I am dangerous
In the dark
Dangerous as the one
Who lights the spark

That feeds your love
Just like a flame
You find I blind and wound
And mame—

'Cause I'm dangerous.

Unavailable

I hope you understand what this means,
That
Emotionally,
I'm unavailable.

Though most of the time
It seems my heart
Is open,
And assailable.

I have closed it off.
Removed, unashamed.
You may pry and scoff.
Yet all you know is my name.

Closed. Removed,
Indeed it is true.
So don't come to me
With persuasion so smooth.

You see where I stand.
My cards are on the table.
The issue at hand is
I'm unavailable.

Uncertainty

A humble beginning—
    With underpinnings
        Of doubt.

How hard I work to root it out!

What Do I Do?

What do I do
When my missing you
Is as broad as the earth?

When a thousand emotions
Erupt into oceans
Of celestial commotion—

Oceans birthing confusion
And a profusion of feelings,
Until I am reeling.

It's an abusive thing,
The perpetual sting of love,
Pining away.

I'm dining on your absence today
And feeling quite
As if I've no appetite.

Where is the Hope?

I've known days—
Days upon days,
And the staring—
I've known man
And his ways of not caring:
Lip-service, lies, promises of doing—
Promises made by those pursuing self-servient desires,
(Politicians, self-proclaimists, liars).

And oh, how the people do tire!
I wonder how people cope.
In this world full of people,
Somewhere,
There has to be hope.
. . . Somewhere

The Beautiful, The Lonely

We dive into the extraordinary
As if it were corn beef hash.
We liquidate our cash
With an eccentric foray of expenditure,
Create a cache for everyday,
And dispose of the mundane
The ordinary,
As if it were trash.

Lives adorned
In cafes and corners,
Full of sashays and foreigners
Intriguing and rare,
Yet, plentiful.

Still, we crawl home,
The dutiful,
Both empty and full.
The beautiful
The lonely.

Looking for Me

You are agreeable—
It's true.
Your life is not
All about you . . .
But it suits your goals.

All else takes a
Bitter toll
And leaves you
Extending . . .
And waiting for
An ending.

You listen,
But it isn't heard.
The anger—
The absurdness
Of who I am

Bounces off the walls
And others see . . .
While I continue
Looking
For me.

Desire

A Hunger—
    But for what
    I can't be sure.

A Longing fills me,
    Vacant and Obscure—
    Distant... but Ever Present.

I think of you
    And how you,
    In your Hunger, pursue me.

Hungrily, you take me in.
    Devouring who I've been
    And where I'm going.

Knowing you can fill me,
    Sensing how you still my mind,
    How I relax and unwind in your presence.

But it's been a long time
    since...

    And now, all I know
    Is this
        Hunger.

Sudden Hush

Words I collect, to give to you,
Come quickly, in a rush.
But one moment in your presence
Seems there comes a sudden hush

Completely blanketing the room.
The effect is very warm.
The sound is ought but silence,
Like the calm before a storm.

Silence, filling every space—
And I sense it. You can tell.
Written on my face
Are words you know all too well.

I sense it's better not to speak them
For fear it would suffice
To remove a guise
Blanketing a heart—as cold as ice.

I Imagine

What it must be like to kiss you
I look at you and imagine—
And wonder.
I'd like to kiss you.

I've traced your face
In my imagination, with my eyes.
And you never knew.
I'd like to touch you.

How it must feel
To wrap you up
In my arms!
I'd like to know it.

How I feel
When you're around
me.
I'd like to show it.

So no reason to question
Why
When a mirror for our soul
Is here, in our eyes.

With His Eyes

I can sit and wait.
I can aggravate this longing
Or I can charm and captivate,
I can mediate
my own belonging.

With what group,
With what pack do I run?
Surely, all under the sun
Are asked
To do God's bidding.

It is, then,
Only ourselves
We are kidding
When we,
As round pegs
Don't fit
Into a square hole,

When we are allotted
Limited control
Of our own destiny
While we peer into
The future
It is only
With His eyes
We see.

Anticipation

"It's going to be wonderful" I said.
"You and me and all these wonderful
Words in my head!"

And indeed I deem it to be—
The world—a fascinating place
When you're with me!

Beauty

Beauty . . .
Ask the beholder.
It's not being younger or older
Than one certain number!

Beauty . . .
The impression I'm under
Is, it is like a natural wonder—
Likened to lightning or thunder.

Beauty . . .
Call it the end of a season—
When leaves cover the earth.
And for rejoicing, a reason—Life itself—

A new birth!

Rain . . .
As I lie there and listen—
Outside, the world, how it glistens
After a summer storm . . .
A breeze on my face that is warm.

I Learned of You

I see every detail of your face.
You were with me—
In another time and place,

Where I learned of you
What I never knew—
I see how much you care.

I feel very close to you.
Tell me—
What should I do?

For now I see
What I did not know of me—
I see how much I care.

I see your hand in mine.
You were with me—
In another place and time.

I know you will always be
In the very heart of me.
You make life seem so fine.

I don't know where you are.
Last night
I wished upon a star.

The nearby moon
Seemed to answered soon
And said you were not far.

It's Over

Let me hear you say,
"It's over."

No other word
Escaping from your lips.

Let me hear you face it.
It's time to come to grips.

Let me hear you say,
"It's over."

For you hold too tight to love—
With fist clenched, as a vise.

Far too much stroking
Finds our love choking, close to death.

If but two words exist
Seek them.

If but with a kiss of death you speak them—
Let me hear you say, "It's over."

Martha

She spoke—
With the grace of God
Imparting.
The very air around her
Started to improve.

You Come to Me

You come to me
With verbiage
Dripping from your lips.

You come to me
With little
Slips of paper.

You call on me
Offering favors
And promises to keep, sweetly.

But can't you see?
I'm not in it that deeply.

Can't you see?
I'm not in it that deeply.

You Must Be of God

What is it about you?
Is it the shape of your face?
Or the way I want so much
To trace it with my eyes,

To send a vision of you
Into infinity
So you will always
Be with me?

For I will live forever.
My God above has promised.
And so can you!
Come and live with me in infinity.

For something as beautiful
As you,
Surely,
Can only be of God.

Touched by Fate

So much time and space—
So separate a life we're living.
And yet, I live to see your face.
I dream of the joys to be given.

One simple hand outstretched,
Reaching to brush your cheek.
These thoughts of mine, not too far fetched,
Feel furious and bleak.

Yet within there shines a light—
A light that your smile emanates
Knowing that life is full and ripe,
And how we've been touched by our fate.

The Pain

It lingers. At times, it is worse. At times, like ocean waves that rise and fall, it rolls in on me, threatening to wash over and drown me. At times, to leave me drenched with emotion, feeling the overpowering pull of its current inside of me: the turmoil. At any time the sound of its awesome potential resonates. I fear the knowing look of others as my futile efforts fail to disguise its evidence. Regardless of the warning, it comes trickling down. No guise will suffice to hide it. Not even from myself. "Pain was never the intention," you once said. Yes. I know. But how could we have known, then? How could we have known?

A Call to Harvest

Words, ready for harvest-
Like grapes, hung about the mind,
Growing, hanging full and ripe,
Poetry on the vine.

Come, oh poet
Make the sweetest wine
For our drinking.
Tell us what you're thinking.

Where the Birds Are

He said he'd take me to a place
Where the birds are—
A place not terribly far
from reality,

Where the door to my heart
Stands ajar—
Where all my emotions
rush out of me.

Five thousand birds in this place!
Birds—Or an extension of me?
Emotions I can't seem to face—
Emotions—alive in the trees.

The mood on that night: wet and weary;
The ground, newly softened by rain.
And so with my soul—sad and teary—
Newly cried tears for my pain.

The sky hung heavy—
for over its shoulders, a dark and dreary cloak.
But for a slight shade of pink and red
The sky could have seemed full of smoke.

To someone disillusioned, as I had been.
In a world full of unassuming men,
Or so it had seemed.
Now this place seemed akin to some of my dreams—

Troubled dreams, where,
surrounded by him,
Determined is he to get in.

To get into my space
Like the birds in this place.
Am I a possession to win?

"What is my value?" I question,
wondering who can impart
solution, remedy, suggestion
for this aching hole in my heart.

Are the birds in this place a part
Of emotions that sped from my soul
Through the door left ajar to my heart?
Now I vow to remove as a whole.

I will not give my heart
Before the trampling herd.
But in all ways be vigilant
And careful of my words.

I will not cast my pearls
before the swine
Nor lay my jewels in the trough
Where they dine.

Of another's judging words
And condemnation, I'll be free.
I will close the door that stands ajar
And give my heart to me.

Resolution

I went back to that place today
But the birds had flown away.
The sky had cleared, and all I had feared
Had vanished in the rays.
Beautiful rays of sunlight
Liquid light, cleansing my soul.
New light I claim as mine—
Filling me up as a whole.
And just as I noticed the birds were gone,
A beautiful sparrow flew in—
Reminding me of God's promises.
They will not toil, or spin.
I'm walking on new ground
My feet planted firm
I pray for his guidance and will.
And with this resolve
I have peace within.
I am comforted, quieted still.
For the door to my heart
That once stood ajar
Circumspect to a world full of sin
Is guarded against the world
And its scars
For my savior is living within.

ROBYN WALLACE KILPATRICK

My Gift of Words for Always

A gift of words—
I'll paint them
Like no picture ever heard.

Wrap them in a faded blue
And give this gift I made
To you.

Brought in
On the wind—
Flown across expanse of sky.

Time and place—
Separate space
Can't break these bonds and ties.

Distance can't separate.
Fate has brought us
To the brink.

And the way fate has brought us
Has prompted me
To think these thoughts.

So I want you to know them,
Always.

For not always will I be around.

But in my love
I hope you've found
A resting place.

And regardless of distance,
Time and Space,
You'll embrace these words

And place them in your heart
There,
Where none can erase.

SHORT STORIES

The Illumination

1 266 Madison Avenue. The mere mention of the address conjures a host of memories, some blurred with strangely muffled voices and others crisp and clear with sharp sound. If I listen closely I can still hear my mother calling us to dinner from Ms. Viola's house. "Ma-a-a-r-k! Ro-obyn!" (Almost with certainty she knew we were next door). Only a sloping mound of earth and a sprawling, old oak separated us from our neighbors, the Rankins. Beyond the oak lay their house and yard with the cherry trees we used to climb, promising wonderfully tart cherries, and a garden as long and wide as a child could imagine. I still see row upon row of furrows ready for the seed. Most of our summers were spent there, a most welcoming place.

One summer, however, stands apart from all others with great distinction: as distinctly as a mother knows her own child, as the seasons differ, and the separation of black and white by prejudice. The disturbing effects of such prejudice would leave an indelible impression on me that summer, forever altering my perception of the world as I knew it to encompass the bitter cruelty of racism.

On most days, I'd find Ms. Viola Rankin on her screened-in porch with a large basket of beans from her garden, to string. On other afternoons, Mom and Ms. Viola would talk while stringin' beans, as I listened and watched. I never could discern which was more important, the conversation or the stringin' of beans, but I liked them both. They were the most comfortable of things, like Ms. Viola. Why, she didn't seem to mind about most things—like having company; or that her hands were wrinkly, like her face; or even that some of her teeth were missing. No, she didn't seem to mind at all. In fact, she was very pleasant most days about most things, and the way she wore her salt and pepper braids made a perfect frame for all that pleasantness.

Without a doubt the Rankins were our favorite neighbors. That summer, however, I became aware that perhaps everyone did not feel the same way about John and Viola Rankin. There was an indescribable tension in the air, a strong stir, an undercurrent of anger. Perhaps I never thought much about what seems now to have been a distinct division of color lines that existed on our block. To the left of the Rankins and all the way up the street were our African-American neighbors, (I recall a different word being used, but it never sounded very nice). To the right of the Rankins, starting with our house, was a newly-developed section. All the residents were white. I didn't think it strange that my father, a Baptist minister, welcomed all races into his congregation every Sunday. Perhaps I wasn't aware that the neighbors on our side of the street did not visit often, and further, that it should be of special interest when Ms. Viola would visit us with squash casserole and bags of fresh vegetables from her garden. Indeed, 1972 was a summer of awakening for a child of seven years.

The hours preceding those of the fateful night were much like other evenings. We were all tucked in, asleep, when I heard the noise—sounds of gunshots followed by shattering glass. I awakened, startled, immediately seeing an extraordinarily bright light outside my bedroom window. It was unlike anything I had seen before, and looking closer I could discern a cross in the center of a huge mass of flame. Someone had placed a cross against the tree which adjoined our property to the Rankin's! At this point, my Mom and Dad rushed in with my brother and pulled me to the floor, shouting, "Stay down! Stay down!" My father directed us to remain in the hallway to avoid being shot. Only he remained there, crouched by that window with the steel tip of his rifle pressed against it. More shouts issued, as well as raucous laughter, but we heard no more gunshots. The ensuing moments were ones of terror as we waited for the police and firemen to arrive. We later discovered no one had been hurt throughout the incident. It was simply a cruel display of hatred for us, and for the Rankins.

Summer afternoons spent with a neighbor, immersed in conversation and sharing in common duty are rare, indeed. Today's frantic pace seems to reduce us to voiceless, nameless neighbors going to and fro, engaged in numerous activities for our own betterment. Many times as I sense the emptiness there, I think back to my childhood spent at 1266 Madison

Avenue. Ms. Viola has a voice in my memory, one that is crisp and clear with sharp sound. She speaks to me of company, sharing, and neighboring but mostly of simple and honest humanness. The only darkness resides in the memory of the horrific act committed that night. Years later, I still vividly recall the fire, and how the flames lept so furiously. It is hard to extinguish the memory of that fire which illuminated every part of me, at seven years of age, to the brutal horror of racism. Today I am aware of the flame, and how we as a people still fight to quench it.

A Time to Rejoice

"Hello Josephine. How do you do? Do you remember me like I remember you? You used to laugh at me and holler, 'Woo, woo, woo!" (Domino). It was 1968, the year my grandmother, Josephine Shelley (Nanny), taught me to "twist" by the old record player. I see her most often that way, in my mind's eye, with that coy tilt to her lovely head and a laugh so free and unrestrained you could roll around in it. At times she would bend double with laughter, barely managing to keep from wetting her pants. She was joy, inventiveness, and love unconditional. Losing her mother at the age of three, she later became the source of love and mothering to others.

Undoubtedly, she could make the best chicken and dumplings and pan of biscuits, but nobody could dish up the stories of the Shelleys like my Nanny. As a child, I would lie awake for hours listening to her unravel her yarn. I can hardly remember a story she told me without the ability to recall the lesson within.

Yes, the lessons conveyed to her grandchildren were many, and the heritage she instilled remains a deep legacy. Within her life, however, Nanny also presented an example of prayer activated and a spirit convicted.

Of life I gleaned a harvest of richest wisdom from Nanny, but the most simple example she taught us will never leave me. It is, that to love most deeply, we must relinquish that which, in the end, belongs to Him.

Until the age of 82, Nanny remained an essential bright and clever existence in our lives, but her light began to fade. From October to December 1995, Nanny was hospitalized on three separate occasions for complications of congestive heart failure. Distraught with the knowledge we could lose her at any moment, our lives began to revolve around her hospital bedside. On several occasions, awakened by urgent phone calls in the middle of the night, we would again visit the cold gray hospital room where intravenous drugs dripped slowly into tubes, supporting the last days of her fragile life. On the morning of December 5, the grave decision was made to remove all life support. She would not live another day.

Between each breath Nanny took we had counted the seconds, but now lay an eternity. Each of our souls seemed to be straining at what remained of Nanny's life. We had to let her spirit go. Joining hands we prayed for God to receive her into his care. Shortly thereafter, we could all feel the overwhelming loss of this moment, the very moment I had dreaded, the day all of us had feared so greatly. Nanny had been all of life to us, but looking at her now, it was hard to believe that what I saw was ever our Nanny. The lifeless body, the house in which her spirit had dwelt for 82 years, was merely a corpse now, an empty shell. Without the vicarous force that gave light to her eyes and the expressive grace indicative only of Josephine Shelley, there was no need to remain in that room. My mother, in her reluctance to leave, hovered over Nanny, smoothing back the soft gray hair from her stiffening forehead. "We can go now mom," I said gently. "Nanny is not here. Surely, she is rejoicing with the angels in heaven."

With only the memory of Nanny, we left that room, relinquishing that which, after all, belongs to Him.

Work Cited

Domino, Fats. *My Girl Josephine.* EMI Records. 1960.